A GUIDE TO THE

PHOTOGRAPHIC

IDENTIFICATION

OF INDIVIDUAL

WHALES BASED

ON THEIR

NATURAL AND

ACQUIRED MARKINGS

JON LIEN AND STEVEN KATONA

 The American Cetacean Society

 Breakwater

Breakwater
100 Water Street
P.O. Box 2188
St. John's, Newfoundland
Canada
A1C 6E6

The American Cetacean Society
P.O. Box 2639
San Pedro, California 90731
U.S.A.

Breakwater gratefully acknowledges the financial support of The Canada Council and of the Cultural Affairs Division of the Department of Municipal and Provincial Affairs, Government of Newfoundland and Labrador, which has made this publication possible.

Canadian Cataloguing in Publication Data

Lien, Jon, 1939-

A guide to the photographic identification of individual whales based on their natural and acquired markings

Includes bibliographical references.
Co-published by the American Cetacean Society.
ISBN 0-920911-89-7

1. Whales—Identification—Handbooks, manuals, etc.
2. Photography of animals—Handbooks, manuals, etc.
I. Katona, Steven K. II. American Cetacean Society.
III. Title.

QL737.C4L53 1990   599.5   C90-097545-8

Contents

Preface

The idea for this book began with a disagreement between the authors about how to photograph blue whales. Was the photo-identification catalogue based on photos of the whale's left or right side? The disagreement broadened! Were fluke photos used for identification of gray whales? Who catalogued bottlenose dolphins on the west coast of the U.S.?

As we talked further, we realized that our own uncertainties demonstrated the need for a quick reference guide which summarized instructions on the photo-identification of cetaceans. We resolved to write it together.

Preparing this book has been very enjoyable and we would like to acknowledge the people who made it that way. Lisa Dugan helped us develop an early draft. John Eastcott, who knows how to take pictures of whales better than the rest of us, agreed to provide photographic advice. Patty Warhol of the American Cetacean Society (ACS) and Robbins Barstow of the Cetacean Society International (CSI) cheered us on at important times. We thank the many investigators who reviewed and criticized early drafts describing their catalogues and provided us with the photographs used in this book, including: Beverly A. Agler, Michael G. Bigg, Dawn Breese, Peter J. Bryant, John Calambokidis, R.H. Defran, Ellie Dorsey, Graeme Ellis, Scott Kraus, Susan Kruse, Susan Lafferty, Steve Leatherwood, Roger Payne, Judith Perkins, Keith Rittmaster, David J. Rugh, Richard Sears, Bernie Tershy, Victoria Thayer, William A. Watkins, Brad Weigle, Mason T. Weinrich, Randall S. Wells, and Bernd Würsig. In addition, we are thankful for the illustrations of Kristine Koch and the late Don Wright.

Sherryl Taylor, Patricia Warhol, and Judy Astone of ACS, Tricia Hayden of Hayden Design and Production, and Clyde Rose of Breakwater Books transformed a print-out from our computers and a pile of pictures into the form of this book. We are very grateful for their efforts.

Jon Lien
Ocean Studies and Psychology
Memorial University of Newfoundland
St. John's, Newfoundland, Canada
A1C 5S7

Steven Katona
College of the Atlantic
Bar Harbor, Maine 04609 USA

Introduction

PHOTO-IDENTIFICATION

During the past two decades the study of living cetaceans using benign (non-harmful) techniques has developed rapidly, and has considerably extended our knowledge of these animals. Photo-identification is based on the fact that individual whales, dolphins, and porpoises

exhibit unique natural and acquired markings which remain the same over time. Markings may have a genetic basis, or may be caused by parasites (such as whale lice or barnacles), predators (such as sharks or killer whales), fights with others of the same species, or by entanglement in ropes or nets, or collision with ships. Whatever their cause, these markings, when photographed, provide the basis for one of the greatest wildlife "tagging" studies of all time.

While it seems obvious that natural markings of animals could be used for individual identification, systematic efforts to photograph and identify cetaceans did not begin until the early 1970s. Gray whales, right whales, humpback whales, and killer whales were species investigators used to develop collections of photo-identified individuals.

Progress has been steady in the nearly 20 years since these tentative beginnings. Catalogues of photographs of identified individuals have grown rapidly for some species and areas. For example, almost 4,000 NW Atlantic humpbacks have been photo-identified, or about 80% of the population in that area. All of the killer whales off the west coast of North America have been identified, and long-lasting family groups can be recognized. Each year at scientific meetings, researchers tell of new species in new locations that are being studied using photo-ID methods.

Part of the reason for the rapid development and success of these photo catalogues has been the photos and data contributed to scientific investigators by many interested volunteers. Good quality photographs, when submitted to investigators with date and location data, are extremely useful in the scientific study of whales.

This book is designed to give you the information you need to photograph properly the cetaceans you encounter and to contribute copies of your photos to a scientific project. Even if you don't take pictures of cetaceans, we encourage you to learn about the research efforts that are described here and to support them in any way you can.

USES OF PHOTO-IDENTIFICATION

A standard method biologists use to study wildlife populations is to apply artificial tags or "marks" to individuals and then follow their activities. Such studies provide information on the animals' movements, associations between individuals, the sequence and timing of events in the life cycle, and even the size of the population. The markings that are used in photo-ID studies are natural "tags" which allow the same sort of studies.

Humpbacks, for example, are seen in northern waters feeding in groups of 2 to 8 animals which sometimes exhibit coordinated movements and perhaps cooperation. Which animals participate in these cooperating groups? Do these groups remain the same? If you can identify individuals, these questions can be answered. Hal Whitehead found that feeding humpback groups are short-lived in Newfoundland; individuals that participate cooperatively may change from group to group. Scott Baker observed, however, that Pacific humpbacks sometimes stayed together for longer periods and occasionally even maintained feeding associations over several years.

In contrast, the work of Mike Bigg and his colleagues in British Columbia and Washington state shows that killer whales live in permanent family groups. Photographs of those animals document every birth and every major change in group composition for nearly a 20-year period. As photograph catalogues expand over the years, we may find other species of cetaceans which exhibit similar social organizations.

Another use of photo-ID information is to track the movements of animals. Using photographs of individually identified humpbacks and dates and locations of resightings, the annual migration cycle of these whales can be charted. The map on page 8 shows that humpbacks photographed in northern feeding areas of the western North Atlantic Ocean during summer return to warm waters in the West Indies for winter.

Photo-ID also provides a way to census a population of whales. The percentage of resighted whales helps scientists estimate the number of individuals in the population.

As catalogues of identified whales are maintained over long periods of time new information will result. A recent example is information on the birthing intervals of female humpbacks. Many humpbacks are now individually identified shortly after birth. This gives scientists the opportunity to study known age whales over the animals' entire lifetimes.

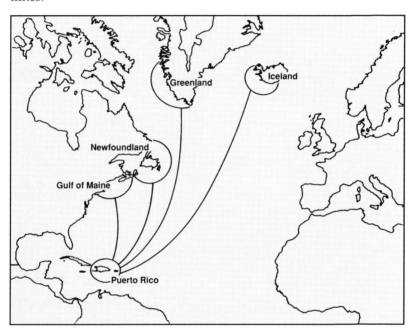

NATURAL AND ACQUIRED MARKINGS

The main requirements for useful individual identification photographs are good, clear pictures accompanied by date and location. Exactly what you photograph will vary with different species. Identification photos generally use a variety of natural and acquired marks.

Humpback fluke showing natural pigmentation patterns.

Humpback fluke showing parallel scars from a killer whale bite.

Callosities on a NW Atlantic right whale.

Dolphin with scars from fighting.

Bottlenose (l) and spinner (r) dolphins with shark bites on dorsal fins.

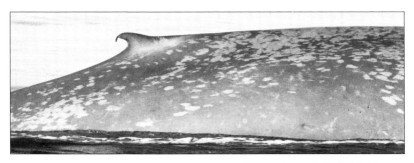

Blotchy pigmentation on blue whales is different in each individual.

A blue whale with scars which may have resulted from scraping on pack ice.

Finback whales have individually unique chevrons and blazes.

Rope scar on a finback dorsal fin.

Male humpbacks acquire scars on their dorsal fin by fighting.

Nobody knows what causes the notches in the trailing edge of sperm whale flukes, but research workers use them to identify individuals.

Photographing Whales

by John Eastcott

In most cases, only a tiny portion of a cetacean's body ever appears above the surface of the sea. Here are some tips to help you turn those short, unexpected moments into useful, memorable photographs.

CAMERA: Use a 35 mm reflex camera, with interchangeable lenses and through-the-lens light meter. On some cameras you can choose different kinds of viewing screens (ground glass, split screen, rings, grid, etc.). Choose a screen that helps you focus crisply and quickly. Power winders or motor drives are very useful. Autofocus lenses may be useful but are still being evaluated. If you plan to purchase a camera, don't be seduced by all the electronic features available on new models. They may be convenient when they work, but more things can go wrong, especially at sea where you can't fix them.

LENS: Most whales are seen at a distance. Lenses shorter than 200 mm focal length are rarely useful, but it is worth bringing a 50 mm lens or short zoom lens just in case a whale adopts your boat. Lenses of 200 mm to 300 mm focal length will capture most photographs and are relatively easy to use. Longer lenses are hard to hold steady on a rocking boat unless you use very fast exposures. Many of today's zoom lenses have excellent optics and provide more flexibility than do fixed focal length lenses. If you don't have a zoom lens, a 1.4x or f2x teleconverter may be used to increase the focal length of a good quality, fairly bright (f4 or faster) fixed length lens. Teleconverters unfortunately decrease the amount of light reaching the film and make focusing harder. Good ones are expensive. Don't buy a cheap one. A good lens shade is a valuable asset in cutting down lens glare. Sky filters (80A) or ultraviolet filters protect the lens from spray. Polaroid filters cut glare, but require frequent adjustment for optimal performance.

FILM: Different research projects have different protocols for film and printing, including colour slides, black and white prints, microscopic inspection of black and white negatives, or colour prints. Colour slides are relatively inexpensive and have excellent resolution. Negative/print films offer greater exposure latitude than slide films and are a good choice for most photo-ID purposes. They also allow you to make copies of photographs easily so that you can send them to research teams. Film speeds of 200 or 400 ASA are generally preferable, since they permit fast shutter speeds and consequently achieve sharper pictures. Kodak T-max 400 ASA is an excellent black and white film and the 400 ASA colour negative films by Fuji and Kodak are both excellent. Higher speed films may be needed for very poor light conditions, but the image will be grainier.

EXPOSURE: Negative films are more tolerant of exposure errors. They are especially forgiving of over-exposure. Most colour slide films only give a good picture if you are within one-half stop of proper exposure. Even through-the-lens meters can be fooled by glare from the sea surface. Be careful not to get too much sky in the picture when taking a light reading. If you do, the sky will photograph nicely, but the whale will be under-exposed. If you are unsure about the proper exposure to use, check your settings with other photographers present. Be sure to set the film speed indicator on your camera to correspond with the ASA rating on the film you load. If your meter fails, a convenient rule of thumb for a sunny day is to set your diaphragm to f/16 and set your shutter speed as close as you can to the ASA rating of the film (e.g. 1/500 sec. for ASA 400 film). Many new cameras have an adjustment to allow for deliberate under- or over-exposure of photographs. These adjustments can be useful, but read your camera manual first. You can also compensate for extraordinary brightness (glare or fog), which would probably fool your camera into the most common exposure problem, under-exposing the dark whale. Another way to do this is with your film speed indicator. For example, if you were using ASA 400 film, you could set the indicator at ASA 200, which would allow more light to enter the camera, making the fog or water seem even brighter than it should, but giving enough light so that the whale would not be under-exposed.

Use sufficiently high-speed film and a large enough lens aperture to allow a shutter speed of at least 1/500 second with a 200 mm lens and 1/1000 second with longer lenses. Only if the boat were very still could slower shutter speeds be used with those lenses, and even then it is risky.

PRACTICING: Become familiar with your equipment before you try photographing whales, otherwise you will be in for a very frustrating experience. Practice setting your camera and focusing as quickly as you can. Choose an object such as a car or tree, then see how fast you can bring the camera to your eye and focus it. Repeat this with different objects at different distances until you can achieve crisp focus within two seconds. Become familiar with the operations of your lightmeter, including automatic or programmed functions. If your camera has those functions, beware of using "aperture-priority" functions which automatically choose a shutter speed to match the f-stop you select. If you stop your camera down too much (choose a small f-stop), the camera will then choose a very slow shutter speed and your image will be blurred. Check your camera settings frequently. Some cameras have knobs that move too easily when brushed accidentally by your finger. Make sure they stay where you want them to.

PHOTOGRAPHING: It takes at least 1/10 second from the time you release the shutter to the time it actually fires. Your reaction time is even longer, so fire slightly before the "perfect moment." If, for example, you do not push the shutter button until a humpback's fluke reaches maximum height, the tail may already be coming down when the image is photographed. Don't bother to shoot a picture unless the whale occupies at least one-third of your view-finder field. If the whale looks like a dot in your view finder, it will only be a dot on your photograph. Do not photograph directly into the sun or the sunstreak on the water.

Separate different rolls of film or different expeditions by photographing a "starter shot" of a piece of paper with information on date, location and roll number. To separate photographs of different whales, it is very important to keep track of frame numbers. This can be difficult for a person working alone since it is hard to photograph and write at the same time. Dictating field notes to a tape recorder will work, but it is far better to have a partner who can keep track of frame numbers and write down observations. Research workers often solve some of these problems by using "data backs" for their cameras. These devices employ light emitting diodes to put date, time of day or other information on each photograph automatically. However, even with a data back it is essential to keep track of the frame numbers representing photographs of each whale. We often separate photo sequences of different whales with "photo blanks," quick shots of the sun (produces a white blank), a hand over the lens (dark blank), or a picture of the boat, a person, a bird or any other non-whale thing. The type of photo blank should be entered in field notes for future reference.

CARE OF EQUIPMENT: Cameras, unlike whales, do not like salt water. Salt water spray shortens the life of a manual camera by corrosion. It also corrodes and shorts out electronic circuits. Whales, by nature, are messy breathers and fill the air with a fine, salty vapour. If a whale is upwind of you and close by, cover your camera before the blow reaches you. Carry tissues or a small towel in your pocket to wipe off spray as necessary. If you expect very wet conditions from spray or rain, bring a clear plastic bag to protect your camera. Wrap it around the camera and lens body, exposing only the front of the lens. Protect your pieces of equipment not in use, such as spare lenses, camera bodies and light meters, by keeping them in a waterproof case or in ziplock plastic bags within your camera bag. Keep film in the plastic waterproof canisters in which it is sold. If you use a motor drive, make sure its batteries are fully charged. Carry a fresh spare of every battery your camera uses. Protect your camera. Even one good dousing can permanently ruin an electronic camera.

COMMON PROBLEMS WITH WHALE IDENTIFICATION PHOTOGRAPHS

The value of photographs which you take can be improved if you avoid a number of obvious problems. Some of these are shown in the following photographs.

Focus here is blurry but the photo may be acceptable for some purposes.

There is glare on the fin which can disguise markings. Also, the timing of this photo is poor and the result is that not enough of the dorsal fin is shown to make this a useful picture.

Again, in this photo the timing is not optimal. The photo was made just a bit too early. The fluke is not vertical, but this photo is still useful for identification.

Just a bit too late! This photo could not serve as primary identification for an animal, but it might confirm a resighting in some cases.

These two photographs of the dorsal fin of the same humpback whale show how important the angle of a photo can be.

Be careful about light. If you shoot into the sun or a bright sky background, the whale will appear uniformly black and its natural markings won't be visible.

Whales do not always cooperate. For example, humpback whales do not fluke up as frequently on their warm-water breeding grounds and a photo like this might be all you can get. If it is clear enough, an identification can still be made.

Good, clear photographs of individually unique traits are necessary to identify an animal. With care, patience, and practice, you can avoid the problems we've described.

MATCHING PHOTOGRAPHS

A critical part of photo-identification is the process of searching a catalogue of identified individuals to see if new photographs "match" any previously-photographed individuals. The investigators and their assistants who maintain scientific collections perform this difficult, time-consuming task. If you photograph whales often in your particular area, you will probably begin matching new photos you take to those of animals you've photographed before. Some people find it easy; others difficult. As the number of identified whales in a catalogue increases, so does the need for patience and care in matching new photographs. Scientists are developing computer-assisted techniques to make matching faster and more efficient, but at the present time the human eye and brain are the best tools that we have for these tasks.

On this page and page 16 are twelve photographs of humpback flukes; two are of the same individual. Can you find them? The answer is on page 77.

1

2

On this page are identification photographs of eight blue whales; two photos show the same animal. Can you find them? The answer is on page 77.

How to Behave Near Whales

There are about 300 right whales in waters off eastern North America, and they may be the only survivors of their species in the entire North Atlantic. They are greatly outnumbered by humans with boats and cameras who would like to see them and take their pictures. Unless we use good judgment, efforts to observe and photo-identify cetaceans can create problems for the whales. The same caution applies to all cetacean species.

Several regions in the United States publish guidelines for whale-watching. Guidelines vary with location because different places and species have different needs. We are still in the early stages of figuring out how we can interact with cetaceans without disturbing or threatening them, so the guidelines are subject to change.

Studying whales using photo-ID may at times entail approaching the animal somewhat closer than normally is permitted under current U.S. regulations or regional guidelines. The U.S. Marine Mammal Protection Act of 1972 may require people doing this type of research to have a permit from the National Marine Fisheries Service. The Canadian government can require a similar permit. Permits may not be necessary in some countries, but photographers should still be courteous to the animals. Since U.S. and Canadian policy is still being developed and refined, it is not yet possible to provide definite advice to photographers. However, the following NOAA fisheries guidelines for the Gulf of Maine, adapted from Beach and Weinrich (1989) appear to be reasonable suggestions to follow in the interim.

A. When in sight of whales (less than 1,500 feet):
   —Avoid excessive speed or sudden changes in speed or direction.
   —Aircraft observe the FAA minimum altitude regulation of 1,000 feet over water.

B. Close approach procedure (less than 600 feet away):
   —Approach stationary whales at no more than idle or "no wake" speed.
   —Parallel the course and speed of moving whales.
   —Do not attempt a head-on approach to moving or resting whales.

C. Multivessel approach (less than 300 feet):
   —All vessels in close approach stay to the side or behind the whales so they do not box in the whales or cut off their path.
   — When one vessel is within 300 feet, other vessels stand off at least 300 feet from the whale.
   —The vessel within 300 feet should limit its time to 15 minutes in close approach to whales.

D. No intentional approach (less than 100 feet away):
   —Do not approach within 100 feet of whales.

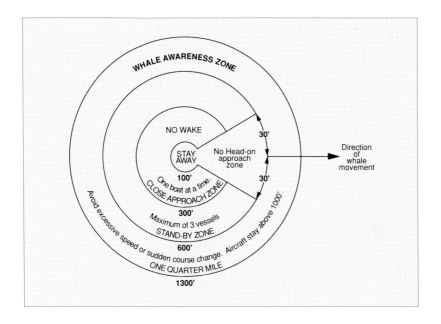

—If whales approach within 100 feet of your vessel, put engine in neutral and do not re-engage props until whales are observed at the surface, clear of the vessel.

Active whales require ample space. Breaching, lobtailing, and flipper-slapping whales may endanger people and/or vessels. Feeding whales often emit subsurface bubbles before rising to feed at the surface. Stand clear of light green bubble patches.

Never restrict the normal movement or behaviour of whales, or take actions that may evoke a reaction from whales or result in physical contact with a whale.

Diving on whales is considered to be an intentional approach of whales and may be considered a violation of federal law.

We do not anticipate that readers of this guide will rush to apply for permits and initiate new photo-ID projects. Instead, we offer it primarily as a source of information for people who might encounter whales during their travels, such as on ferry boats, cruising by sail or motor, fishing, or sea kayaking. Photographs taken in places or at times when scientists are not present can be particularly valuable to the research projects. We hope that this guide will be useful to the whalewatching public by helping to explain some of the work that naturalists and scientists are doing from whalewatch boats.

Using This Guide

Active photo-ID programs exist for at least sixteen species of cetaceans. Some have a relatively long history and large catalogues of identified individuals; others are new efforts. For each species, features to be photographed are slightly different. There usually are several investigators interested in the same species, but working in different locations or oceans. Details of how to photograph are given for each species. Where to send identification photographs begins on page 60. A glossary of whale words and a labelled drawing of a whale can be found on pages 73–76 at the end of the guide.

HOW TO
PHOTOGRAPH
Whales

FOR INDIVIDUAL
IDENTIFICATION

HUMPBACK WHALE
(Megaptera novaeangliae)

Fieldmarks for species identification

- length to 52 ft (18 m); most 35–40 ft (ll–l3 m); birth length 13 ft (4 m)
- black above, mostly white below
- bushy spout up to 15 ft (4.5 m) high
- often slight hump forward of dorsal fin; dorsal fins vary in shape and may be "floppy" or scarred
- long flippers, up to 1/3 body length; Atlantic humpbacks' flippers are white above and below, with some black markings; flippers of Pacific specimens often dark above and below
- knoblike bumps on head visible at close range
- usually raises flukes in air when diving at end of breathing sequence; underside of flukes variably patterned; trailing margin of flukes sawtoothed
- behaviours frequently seen include breaching, pounding water with flippers or tail, lunging out of water while feeding

Natural markings to be photographed: pattern on underside of flukes, dorsal fin, scars or unusual marks on body.

Flukes of four humpbacks. In the photo on the bottom right the angle could make matching difficult. Although only part of the fluke is exposed on the top right photo, a match to a previous photograph was made.

Photographs of four distinctive dorsal fins. Recognition of dorsal fins is especially useful in distinguishing individuals within a group of whales. Photograph dorsal fins at right angles to the whale and be careful to record which dorsal fin corresponds to which fluke photograph.

A humpback's breathing pattern changes with its activities, for example, how deep it is diving. As you become experienced in watching whales, you will be able to anticipate when a deep dive is about to occur so that you can be ready to photograph. The best photographs are those taken squarely behind the whale when the flukes are perpendicular to the camera and completely exposed.

Thanks to the variety of their natural markings and their tendency to fluke up, humpbacks were among the first large whales to be individually identified by photographic "tags." Large-scale systematic collection of fluke photographs has been carried out for over ten years, and has yielded information about population size, population substock structure, migration routes and rates, age at first reproduction, calving frequency, and other important facts.

In addition to fluke photographs, pictures of the dorsal fin, head, and sides of the same whale are very useful. If the whale does not fluke up, photographs of these other body features may still allow it to be identified. Such photographs may also contain other information. For example, on the breeding range humpback males compete for access to females, and their dorsal fins, heads, and bodies may show scars from these confrontations. Photographs of these features may thus give some indication of the whale's sex. Photographs of the genital area are necessary for definite confirmation of sex.

Probably male

Probably female

PROCEDURES FOR SUBMITTING PHOTOGRAPHS

Most collections use black and white prints, but any type of photographs can be used, including colour prints or slides. If photographs are submitted as prints, preferred format is 2.5 x 4 inches overall, with an image size of 2 x 3.5 inches. Each photo should list date, location, photographer's name, and roll/frame numbers if known.

BLUE WHALE
(Balaenoptera musculus)

Fieldmarks for species identification

- average length to 75–80 ft (24 m) for males; 75–90 ft (27 m) for females; maximum reported length 110 ft (33.5 m)
- pale blue-gray to dark gray, always mottled with irregular spots (visible at close range), not always heavily mottled
- strong, straight spout up to 30 ft (9 m) high
- dorsal fin set far back on body and very small
- flippers short, about 1/10 body length, dark above, light below
- about 13% of the time raises flukes in air (maximum angle about 45°) for terminal dive
- seen singly, paired, or in small groups

Natural markings to be photographed: pattern on both sides of body near dorsal fin, dorsal fin, flukes, and any scars or unusual markings.

Complete photographic coverage of an identified blue whale from the Gulf of St. Lawrence, showing left and right sides, dorsal fin, and flukes.

Some blue whales are easy to approach, others difficult. The behaviour of each animal will affect the job of taking identification photos.

The best photographs for ID show as much of each side as possible, including the dorsal fin, so the individually-distinctive mottling pattern is clearly visible. The dorsal fin acts as a point of reference, but it may also be an identification clue if it is unusually shaped, scarred, or deformed.

The best moment to take an ID photo is when the whale is rounding out to dive. Position yourself squarely alongside of the animal, just ahead of the dorsal fin. Oblique photographs distort the marking pattern, making identifications more difficult. Photograph one side of the animal from the head to tail during one or more encounters, then repeat for the opposite side. Terminal dives take several seconds for such a large animal, so you can take several photographs. Motor drives are very useful for these sequences. Dive times can last for up to 20 minutes, so be patient until the whale reappears. Even expert blue whale photographers spend up to an hour getting adequate identification pictures from one whale. Don't try to rush it.

Three different individuals seen from the left side. Compare these photographs with the individual shown previously.

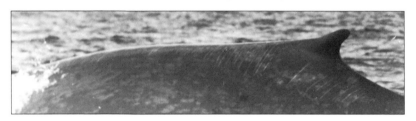

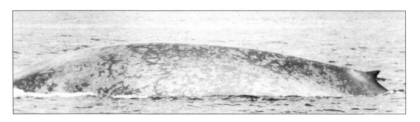

PROCEDURES FOR SUBMITTING PHOTOGRAPHS

Researchers prefer 400 ASA film. Negatives, or photos in a format of 2.5 x 7 in. black and white prints, are requested along with date, location, identification of any associated animals for each particular sighting, photographer's name, and frame/roll number if known.

FINBACK WHALE
(Balaenoptera physalus)

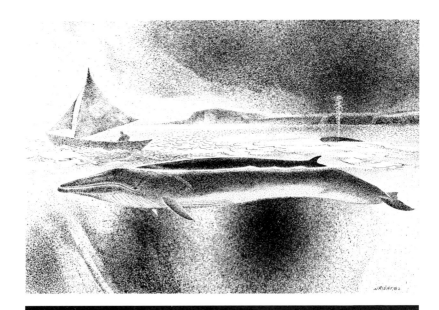

Fieldmarks for species identification

- length from 50–80 ft (21 m)
- dark gray on back, white below
- strong, straight spout up to 20 ft (6 m) high
- relatively large dorsal fin, shape somewhat variable, but usually curved and pointed
- flippers short, about 1/10 body length, dark above, light below
- asymmetric coloration of head is unique to species: right lower jaw and first third of baleen are white, but left lower jaw and all baleen on left are dark
- behind the head a pale gray "V" or chevron can be seen at close range with good viewing conditions; this pattern is particularly noticeable on the right side
- flukes hardly ever raised in air
- often seen in small groups (2–8 whales); sometimes alone

Natural markings to be photographed: colour pattern on both sides of head and extending back along right side; dorsal fin should also be photographed (right side preferred), and any other distinctive scars or body markings.

Three different individuals photographed from the right side. Several photographs of an animal may be required for definite identification.

Dorsal fins of four individuals are shown above. Distinctive shapes, notches or scars on dorsal fins are an important supplement to photos of the head and chevron.

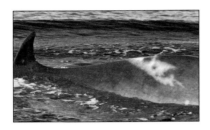

Body scars are also often seen on fin whales and provide identification features which should be photographed.

Photo-ID of finback whales is difficult. They are fast, and it may be hard to position yourself well. Since the whales often swim in pairs or small groups, special effort must be made to keep photos of different whales separate. Identifying features can only be seen at close range since distinctive features are often subtle in this species. Markings such as notches in the trailing edge of the dorsal fin may appear to be unique on first sight, but many whales have them, so excellent photographs are required for definite identification of individuals.

There are different strategies for positioning a boat near a finback whale, depending on the whale's behaviour, sea conditions, etc. On a fine, calm day it is sometimes possible to work with a single animal for an hour or more, and finbacks may approach a boat closely at such times. On other days a long game of hide-and-seek may be required. Under most conditions it is very important to learn the whale's breathing pattern—for example, 7 blows at 15 second intervals followed by an 8 minute dive. With this information the boat operator knows approximately when the whale should surface and how long it will be visible for photography. The best photographs of the head and chevron may be obtained during shallow dives, but the dorsal fin and other scars may only be visible on a terminal dive. The boat must be positioned parallel to the whale's course and to the starboard side of the whale.

Views of the chevrons of two whales. The figure on the left shows the start of the chevrons; the figure on the right shows a complete view of the chevrons.

Photographers must anticipate the surfacing of the whale, pre-focusing the camera on the spot where the animal is likely to come up. Polarizing sunglasses will cut surface glare and may allow the photographer to see the whale rising. Motor-drive photography should begin just before the whale's head breaks the surface and should continue until the whale submerges. A continuous sequence of photographs of the head, chevron, side, and dorsal fin is most useful. This can be done efficiently with a motor-drive camera, but will require a number of dive sequences if a manual-wind camera is used. Photographs from the right side are of primary importance.

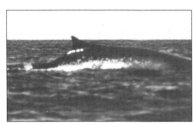

Here are some examples of poor photographs that will not allow positive identification of a finback whale. Backlighting, glare, water splash, and poor timing of the shot will reduce the value of your photographs even if they are properly exposed.

PROCEDURES FOR SUBMITTING PHOTOGRAPHS

Different researchers have different preferences for film type. Photographs in any format will be useful, but colour slides may contain more information. Each photo should list date, location, photographer's name, and roll/frame numbers if known.

MINKE WHALE
(Balaenoptera acutorostrata)

Fieldmarks for species identification

- smallest baleen whale; maximum length 30 ft (9 m), most specimens about 25 ft (7.5 m) or less
- dark back, porcelain white belly; light gray "chest blaze" visible on both sides, forward of dorsal fin, in good light
- weak spout, usually not visible except in cold air
- tall, sharply curved (hooked) dorsal fin, set far back on the body
- conspicuous white band across each short (about 1/10 body length) flipper
- tip of sharply pointed "snout" is often the first thing to break water as whale surfaces to breathe; baleen is pure white
- flukes hardly ever raised in air
- often seen close to shore, alone or in pairs; but also occurs offshore, sometimes in larger groups; usually ignores boats, but may approach stopped vessels; sometimes breaches

Natural markings to be photographed: broadside view of the dorsal fin and as much of the body as possible, from both sides. Several frames of each side are most useful. Show all of the body from just behind the blowholes to the end of the tailstock. A motor drive or power winder on your camera is helpful for this. Scars and the pale "chest blaze" are particularly important features.

Two distinctive minke whales. Identification often requires scars or the pale "chest blaze."

Minke whales are difficult to approach or follow. They are fast and have short breathing sequences—for example, two or three breaths at intervals of 20 or 30 seconds, followed by a dive for 3 minutes or so. Minkes can dive for much longer. We watched one hold its breath for 17 minutes before it broke through the fish weir in which it had become accidentally entrapped. Minke whales sometimes vanish as if by magic. Since the spout is not normally visible, these little whales can easily swim out of range unnoticed by an observer, especially if the water is at all rough.

Such behavioural traits leave little time for careful positioning of a boat. Nevertheless, a boat operator must try to put the photographer broadside to the whale and close enough so that its side will fill as much of the frame as possible. Even if the whale approaches the boat, as minkes sometimes do, it usually occurs without warning and your camera had better be ready because the whale is unlikely to repeat his approach.

If you are lucky enough to come upon a minke that is traveling steadily, getting a photograph is much easier. A traveling minke whale may surface as many as 4 to 7 times in a row between longer dives, and the direction and speed of travel can be quite constant. Sometimes minke whales travel at speeds as low as one knot.

This photograph, which cannot be used for individual identification because of its poor angle, shows that even a close approach does not always result in photos useful for identification. Photography of minke whales requires experience, careful preparation, readiness, and (perhaps above all) luck.

PROCEDURES FOR SUBMITTING PHOTOGRAPHS

Photographic identification of minke whales has been used so far only in local areas, but it has proved useful in documenting the number of individuals in an area, the extent of range occupied by each individual, and the year-to-year return of individuals to an area. Each photo should list date, location, photographer's name, and roll/frame numbers if known.

SEI WHALE
(Balaenoptera borealis)

Fieldmarks for species identification

- ■ length under 50 ft (15 m), specimens normally about 45 ft (13.7 m) or less
- ■ dark back and sides, lighter on belly; light spots may be visible on back or sides when seen at close range; unlike finback whale, both sides of the head are dark in adults
- ■ straight spout up to 15 ft (5 m) high, similar to that of finback whale but not as high; spout about once per minute; surfacing may not be coordinated among individuals
- ■ large dorsal fin set farther forward than in finback or minke, usually sharply hooked and pointed in its upper portion
- ■ flippers all dark and relatively small (1/10 body length)
- ■ flukes dark and hardly ever raised above water
- ■ sei whales swim in an erratic manner, often very fast with frequent changes of direction

Natural markings to be photographed: three photographs of each individual are suggested—one of head/chevron region, one of flank, and one of the dorsal fin. All three photographs should show the same side of the body. Dorsal fin photos should be taken perpendicular to the body, from both sides if possible. Watch carefully for distinctive scars or unusual natural markings since they are particularly important in identifying this species. Photograph them so that their location on the animal can be determined and their pattern clearly seen. Photographs taken from the side of the animal should include the dorsal fin or blowhole as a point of reference.

Four sei whales that appear to be individually distinctive.

The effort to photo-ID sei whales is new, but most animals observed so far appear to be individually identifiable by the three-photo sequence. Little detailed information is available on the seasonal distribution of the species or on how individuals react to research boats. As with any wild animal, it takes time for an observer to learn the behaviour of the individual and for the animal to (perhaps) become accustomed to the vessel. Record your observations of behaviour so that you will be able to use that information in the future or contribute it to researchers.

PROCEDURES FOR SUBMITTING PHOTOGRAPHS

All photographs are of interest. Black and white 3 x 5 in. prints are preferred. Each photo should list date, location, photographer's name, and roll/frame numbers if known.

RIGHT WHALE

(Eubalaena glacialis)

WRIGHT '87

Fieldmarks for species identification

- adult length to about 50 ft (15.2 m)
- adults black above, with white patches below; some have white scars on the back; some individuals are light or gray; calves often lighter
- spout to 10 or 15 ft (5 m) in calm air; spout shape "bushy"; wide separation of nostrils causes spout to have clearly divided V-shape when seen from fore or aft
- no dorsal fin
- large head, 1/4 length of fat, stocky body, bears long (to 11 ft, 3.5 m) dark baleen; at close range top and front of head have rough lumpy protrusions called "callosities"; callosities are mainly white because they are covered with hundreds of white whale lice (cyamid amphipods); some patches are colored yellow or orange by other species of whale lice

(continued)

- wide, black flukes have pointed tips, deep median notch and smooth trailing edges; light scars on ventral surface can be useful for individual identification; flukes are raised high in air for terminal dive
- seen singly, in pairs, or in groups of up to 10 whales; behaviours seen include breaching, "sleeping" at surface, skim feeding, courtship groups; other interesting behaviours to watch for include hanging head-down and using tail for "sailing," curiosity about moored or floating objects in water, and interaction with gulls, seals, dolphins, or pilot whales

Natural markings to be photographed: pattern of callosities on head; unusual scars or markings on body; crenulations, or unique edge patterns, along the upper margin of the lower lips.

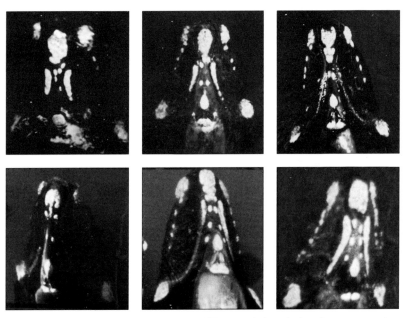

Aerial photographs of heads of six different right whales from coastal waters near Argentina, showing how individuals may be distinguished by pattern of callosities on the head.

Photographs of four North Atlantic right whales taken from small vessels.

Individual right whales are identified primarily by photographs of the size, shape, and relative positions of callosities on their heads. Callosities are found along the upper jaw, rostrum, around the blowhole, along the sides of the lower jaws, and on the "chin." Several species of cyamids (whale lice) occur on the callosities, each occupying a preferred habitat on the head. White cyamids frequently occupy the convex callosities. Orange, pink, or yellow whale lice are more often seen on indentations, edges of callosities, fresh wounds, and genital areas. Although individual cyamids can wander around the skin, most remain in place so that the apparent shape of the callosities changes very little. Since callosity patterns are three dimensional, numerous photographs from all angles are helpful in identification. Photographs of body scars or markings should also be obtained. Crenulations along the upper margin of the lower lips, the callosity patterns that occur just behind the blowholes, and scarring on the tailstock, flukes, and fluke-tips are important.

Unusual scars or body markings can also be useful in photo-identification of right whales. Scars on the fluketips are common.

PROCEDURES FOR SUBMITTING PHOTOGRAPHS

South Atlantic researchers photograph from airplanes or cliffs with either black and white or color slide film. Photographs are utilized primarily as black and white prints. North Atlantic scientists work mainly from small boats and use colour slides. Photographs in any format can be submitted. Each photo should list the date, location, photographer's name, and frame/roll number if known.

GRAY WHALE
(Eschrichtius robustus)

Fieldmarks for species identification

- adult length to 46 ft (14 m)
- dark gray skin becomes mottled over time with many white spots, rings, and patches; at close range, many large white barnacles and orange clusters of whale lice (cyamid amphipods) are visible in large individuals
- low "bushy" or heart-shaped spout, usually V-shaped when seen from front or rear
- no dorsal fin, instead a blunt "hump" followed by a series of knobs or knuckles along the back all the way to the flukes
- broad, gray flukes frequently marked and scarred, raised in the air before a deep dive
- coastal or inshore; closely follow coastline during some parts of migration; may be seen singly, in pairs, or in groups of up to 10 animals or more

Natural markings to be photographed: pattern of scarring or marking on sides of body in area surrounding dorsal hump. The profile of "knuckles" on the dorsal ridge of the back is also useful.

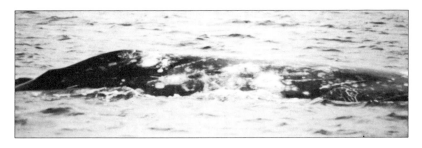

Photographs of four different gray whales, above, show how individuals may be distinguished by body scarring patterns.

The knuckle profile on the dorsal ridge is also an individually distinct characteristic.

Fluke photographs of gray whales can be used for individual identification. Be sure to keep careful records so photographs of flukes and sides of the same individuals can be grouped reliably. Obtaining photographs of the whale's left side, right side, and flukes will require several breathing sequences.

The gray whale was one of the first baleen whales to be individually-identified on the basis of natural markings. Jim Darling's and David Hatler's repeated sightings of distinctively-marked gray whales proved that some animals returned to feed along the coast of British Columbia during different years. One of the problems that confronts anyone using photo-ID on gray whales is the size of the gray whale population. With an estimated population of 20,000 whales, there is low probability for resighting a whale unless individuals return each year to specific parts of the breeding or feeding ranges.

PROCEDURES FOR SUBMITTING PHOTOGRAPHS

Each photo should list the date, location, photographer's name, and frame/roll number if known.

KILLER WHALE
(Orcinus orca)

Fieldmarks for species identification

- length to 30 ft (9.1 m) for males; about 25 ft (7.6 m) for females
- body black above except for oval white patch just above and behind each eye and grayish "saddle" on back below and behind dorsal fin; underside mostly white
- spout is visible in cool air, up to 10 ft (3 m) high
- dorsal fin very tall to 6 ft (1.8 m) and triangular in males, smaller 2.5 ft (0.8 m) and more rounded in females
- flippers large, black, round at ends
- usually seen in small groups of 3 to 30 animals; behaviours observed include breaching, spyhopping, slapping water surface with tail or flippers; occasionally seen eating fish or hunting whales, seals, or birds

Natural markings to be photographed: dorsal fin and gray saddle on both sides. Many researchers concentrate on the left side in order to reduce the number of photographs needed and to avoid possible confusion.

On the left, two female killer whales from British Columbia; on the right, two male killer whales from the same area.

To photograph killer whales, position your boat slightly behind and parallel to the animals. The most experienced photographers suggest that you should be 100 to 200 ft (30 to 60 m) from the whales. Adjust your speed to slightly greater than that of the whales. Remember that the standard is to photograph the whales on their left side. The reason for this is the asymmetrical differences in the pattern of the gray saddle. There are enough distinctive features in a photo of one side of a killer whale to permit individual identification. Photographs of the left and right sides will not be identical and good field notes are required for matching. Taking pictures only of the left side reduces the amount of work by half and eliminates a possible source of confusion. Don't despair if you are only able to photograph an animal on its right side. The photograph may still be useful if the animal has a distinctively shaped dorsal fin (which will probably be nearly identical when seen from either side) or a scar; it is also possible that a right side photograph already exists for the animal that may allow a match to be made.

Because killer whales have been photographed so extensively in the Pacific Northwest since 1970, there is good evidence that their natural markings remain consistent. This is particularly important since calculations indicate killer whales live a long time.

Individuals can usually be identified by the pattern of the gray dorsal saddle. There is evidence that general sizes and shapes of the dorsal fin differ between two apparent races of killer whales in the Pacific Northwest. The "resident" race travels in local coastal ranges; "transient" pods may spend most of their lives in the open ocean. Further, there are differences between residents of different areas.

Shape of transient pod dorsal fin.   **Shape of resident pod dorsal fin.**

PROCEDURES FOR SUBMITTING PHOTOGRAPHS

Photos in any format accepted, along with date, location, photographer's name, and frame/roll number if known.

SPERM WHALE
(Physeter catadon)

WRIGHT '82

Fieldmarks for species identification

- largest toothed whale; males 40–55 ft (12–17 m); females 25 to 38 ft (7.5–12 m)
- body dark gray or brown color with "wrinkled" skin
- blowhole on front of head, to left of midline so that "bushy" spout (to 15 ft, 5 m) is tipped forward and to left in still air; may spout 20 to 50 times before diving for up to an hour
- low, blunt dorsal fin; many females have distinct callus on leading edge of dorsal fin, but this is absent in males; behind the hump is a row of "knuckles" running down the ridge of the back
- "square head" shows above water when whale blows
- wide, heart-shaped flukes often raised into the air during a terminal dive
  (continued)

■ behaviours seen include breaching, pounding water with flukes, sleeping at surface, lying motionless at surface; may occur singly, but more often seen in groups of up to 20 or more animals, especially in the tropics

Natural markings to be photographed: flukes

Flukes from four different sperm whales showing distinctive natural marks and scars. These photographs are from the Galapagos Islands.

Sperm whales are usually found well offshore in deep water, so few people get the opportunity to see and photograph them. Photographs of the underside of the flukes can be obtained when the animal makes a terminal dive, pounds the water with its tail, or turns sharply with one side of the flukes out of the water. Photographs should be taken at distances less than 100 m, in good light, with a telephoto lens of focal length 300 mm or more. Individual flukes vary in a number of characteristics. The edges of some flukes are very rough or notched and many have scars, holes, barnacles, and goose barnacles. Distinctive marks or scars on other parts of the body should also be photographed. Indications of the sex of an individual can be shown by photographs of the head and dorsal fin. The head of a large male is more square and massive than that of a female; and only females appear to have calluses on the leading edge of the dorsal hump.

orsal fins of a female (top) showing a callus on the leading edge, and a
1ale (bottom) in which the callus is absent.

ROCEDURES FOR SUBMITTING PHOTOGRAPHS

hoto-identification research on sperm whales has been done using
egatives taken on hi-speed (ASA 400 or more), fine grain black and
hite film. The negatives are examined under a dissecting microscope
nd compared with prints or contact sheets of flukes in a research
atalogue. Black and white negatives are the preferred format, but
hotographs in any format will be welcomed. For each photo list the
ate, location, photographer's name, and roll/frame number if known.

BOTTLENOSE DOLPHIN
(Tursiops truncatus)

Fieldmarks for species identification

- adults to 12 ft (4 m) in length
- body colour dark gray or dusky brown, sometimes with pink tone ventrally, and with pale wash along sides of body; body not spotted
- curved dorsal fin
- robust head; short stout beak forms crease at rise of skull
- typically seen near coast, usually in small groups (less than 50 animals); offshore groups may be larger

Natural markings to be photographed: dorsal fin and sides of body.

Photographs of four different bottlenose dolphins from Florida, distinguished by dorsal fin shape or scars.

Unless observed at close range and under good conditions, the colour of bottlenose dolphins appears to be uniform and featureless. Most individuals are recognizable on the basis of distinctive dorsal fin shapes, or by scars or notches on the dorsal fin. Dolphins are more difficult to photograph than large whales because they are small, fast, show little of themselves above the water, and do not spend long at the surface for each breath. It is often difficult to choose and focus on one dolphin in a group.

Most efforts to photo-ID bottlenose dolphins have been in local areas because individuals appear to confine their movements to a home range. Along the California coastline, however, considerable back and forth movement has been documented. Research projects at several locations in the Southern California Bight, in the southeastern United States, and in the Gulf of Mexico are providing important information about patterns of movement, differences in migration patterns between males and females, and life history.

PROCEDURES FOR SUBMITTING PHOTOGRAPHS

Clear photographs in any format are acceptable. Each photo should list the date and location of the photograph, the photographer's name, and frame/roll number if known.

Identification Photographs of Other Species

You may encounter a distinctively marked cetacean of another species that has not been mentioned so far. Photographs of unusual scars, dorsal fin notches, or colouration patterns may allow for re-identification of individual animals at a later date. In species for which scientists have not accumulated research catalogues, the likelihood of matching the unusual animal you photograph will be quite low. However, submission of the photograph is still valuable for three reasons. First, research collections must start somewhere, and your photo may be useful in the early stages of that process. Second, even if a catalogue is not completed until many years later, your early photograph can provide important retrospective information. Finally, the animal you photograph may be a regular resident or visitor to your area and you may be able to re-identify it on another occasion.

Owing to the scientific success of photo-identification methods, it is likely that research catalogues will be developed for several new species of whales in coming years. Currently there are initial efforts to photo-identify individual white-sided dolphins, bowhead whales, Bryde's whales, local populations of belugas, Risso's dolphins, and spinner dolphins. Short summaries for these species are presented here.

Most investigators are interested in any good, clear photos, identified by name of photographer, location, and date. Addresses of interested researchers are listed beginning on page 60.

WHITE-SIDED DOLPHIN
(Lagenorhynchus acutus)

White-sided dolphins are often seen in groups that range in size from several animals to several thousand animals. They frequently breach and hitch rides in the bow wave of ships or body surf in their wake. These activities provide good photographic opportunities. Mature animals (6-8 ft, 2-2.5 m) have dark backs with a V-shaped saddle which points downward directly below the dorsal fin. Individuals can be identified by scars, variation in pigmentation and variation in the shape of dorsal fins. Dorsal fin nicks and scars, body wounds, and novel pigmentation seem to be most useful. Photos can be either black and white or colour slides.

BOWHEAD WHALE
(Balaena mysticetus)

 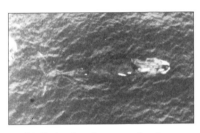

Patches of white pigment on the chin and tailstock, plus acquired scars, allow for individual identification of the four bowhead whales shown in these aerial photographs from Alaska.

Because bowhead whales are almost entirely restricted to the Arctic, not many people have an opportunity to observe and photograph them. To further complicate matters, current individual-identification research relies heavily on photographs taken from aircraft. In body form, these whales look like right whales, but they are larger (up to 55 ft, 17 m), bulkier, and the head is more massive (up to 1/3 body length) and lacks callosities. They have no dorsal fins. Useful natural markings include variable patches of white on the chin and tailstock, as well as acquired scars on the black back and sides of the animals.

BRYDE'S WHALE
(Balaenoptera edeni)

Photographs of scars and markings on the dorsal fin and body surface have permitted studies of habitat use and residency patterns of Bryde's whales in the Gulf of California.

This species is about the size and shape of a sei whale. It is found in warmer waters more often than the other baleen whales. The species is not easy to identify because its main fieldmark can only be seen at close range. All of the other whales in its family (Balaenopteridae)—the blue, finback, sei, and minke—have a single ridge that runs down the midline of the rostrum. Bryde's whale has an additional ridge on each side of the central one, for a total of three parallel rostral ridges. If the rostral ridges cannot be seen, Bryde's whales can be distinguished from fin whales because the leading edge of their dorsal fin forms an abrupt angle. On a fin whale the angle of the leading edge is less abrupt. Little is known about Bryde's whale so any record of its distribution is of value. Therefore, a photograph will be useful even if it does not permit identification of the individual.

BELUGA
(Delphinapterus leucus)

These small whales are restricted nearly entirely to arctic waters. A number of separate beluga populations are spread across the Arctic, but the animals most frequently seen by whalewatchers come from an endangered population in the Gulf of St. Lawrence near the mouth of the Saguenay River. An estimated 5000 belugas once lived there, but severe overhunting during the 1800s and increasing marine pollution are responsible for the population's continuing decline. Only about 300 animals remain, but they can be seen on commercial whalewatch trips that operate in the Saguenay. Individual animals from this population are known to stray into Maine, Massachusetts, and as far south as Long Island, New York. A number of lucky people have had the opportunity to see these unusual individuals during the weeks or months they spend in southern waters. Belugas are easy to identify. They have no dorsal fin. Adults are up to 13 ft (4 m) long, and are pure white. Calves are born gray, and lighten gradually over a period of 5 to 10 years. The head is bulbous with a very short "smiling" beak.

Belugas from Hudson Bay have been photo-identified on the basis of visible scars and other markings on the body.

RISSO'S DOLPHIN

(Grampus griseus)

This large dolphin (length to 14 ft, 4.3 m) is found worldwide in tropical and temperate seas. It is distinguished from other dolphins by the absence of a distinctive beak, absence of teeth in the upper jaw, and 3 to 7 pairs of large, pointed teeth in the lower jaws. These features are not visible from a boat, so whalewatchers must observe the pattern of scars that these animals acquire, apparently from fights with other Risso's dolphins. The scar patterns are distinctive and long-lasting, but taking pictures of them is not easy because the dolphins are small and fast.

As the animal ages, the gray of its upper body is marked by numerous long, white scars; older animals, especially males, are nearly white. The tall, sharply pointed dorsal fin is usually less scarred, often remaining dark in contrast to the lighter body. There is sufficient variation to be useful for individual identification. Risso's dolphins often breach or stick their heads out of the water, giving an opportunity to see much of the body.

Photographs of Risso's dolphins from Monterey Bay, California showing scars and dorsal fin shapes.

There is a study on this species in Monterey Bay, California, using photographs of patterns on the animals' dorsal fins and backs. Resightings over a 15 month period show that most of the markings are stable for at least that amount of time.

SPINNER DOLPHIN
(Stenella longirostris)

These small, streamlined dolphins are quite variable geographically. The only group which has been studied using photo-identification is the Hawaiian population. In Hawaii, spinner dolphins grow to 7 ft (2.1 m) in length. They have long, slender beaks and their bodies are dark gray on top, light gray along the flanks, and white on the belly. The dorsal fin is tall, pointed, and curved. Spinner dolphins get their common name from their habit of jumping and spinning as they swim. No practical use has been suggested for that behaviour. In contrast to other Pacific spinner populations in which the dolphins form herds of up to 1000 animals or more, Hawaiian spinners form local groups of several hundred animals, and often are found with humpback whales. Smaller groups facilitate photo-identification studies. Identified individuals have been studied off Hawaii over a period of years.

APPENDIX I
Where to Submit Photos

LISTED BY SPECIES

HUMPBACK WHALE
Send photographs to:

North Atlantic Region:
Allied Whale
College of the Atlantic
Bar Harbor, ME 04609 USA

Southern Gulf of Maine:
Center for Coastal Studies
P.O. Box 826
Provincetown, MA 02657 USA

Pacific Region:
S.A. Mizroch
National Marine Mammal
Laboratory
7600 Sand Point Way NE
Building 4
Seattle, WA 98115 USA

Australia:
Mark L. Simmons
Queensland National Parks &
Wildlife Service
Maritime Estate Branch
P.O. Box 1362
Rockhampton, 4700
Queensland, Australia

Catalogues:

Katona, S.K., P. Harcourt, J.S. Perkins and S.D. Kraus (eds.) 1980. A catalogue of individuals indentified by fluke photographs. College of the Atlantic, Bar Harbor, Maine 04609. 169 pp. This catalogue is out of print. It shows approximately 1,000 photographically-identified individuals from the North Atlantic Ocean. Since the collection of photos from this region has now grown to nearly 4,000 individuals, it is not practical to publish a complete catalogue in book form. General publication by videodisc may be an option in the future.

Mayo, C., C. Carlson, P. Clapham and D. Mattila. 1985. Humpback whales of the Southern Gulf of Maine. Center for Coastal Studies, Provincetown, Massachusetts, 02657. 62 pp. This catalogue contains photographs of flukes and dorsal fins of approximately 250 whales from the Southern Gulf of Maine. (Available from the Center for Coastal Studies, $12 U.S.)

BLUE WHALE
Send photographs to:

Pacific Region:
John Calambokidis
Cascadia Research
218 West Fourth
Olympia, WA 98501 USA

Sea of Cortez and the North Atlantic:
Richard Sears
Mingan Island Cetacean Study
285 Green Street
St. Lambert, Quebec, Canada
J4P 1T3

Catalogues:

Sears, R., F.W. Wenzel and J. M. Williamson. 1987. The blue whale: a catalogue of individuals from the western North Atlantic (Gulf of St. Lawrence). Mingan Island Cetacean Study, 285 rue Green, Saint-Lambert, Quebec J4P 1T3, Canada. 64 pp.

FINBACK WHALE
Send photographs to:

North Atlantic Region:
  Allied Whale
  College of the Atlantic
  Bar Harbor, ME 04609 USA

Pacific Region:
  Bernie Tershy and Dawn Breese
  Section of Neurobiology and
  Behavior
  Mudd Hall
  Cornell University
  Ithaca, NY 14853 USA

Catalogue:
The effort to collect and curate collections of photographs of finback whales is quite new. No published catalogue.

MINKE WHALE
Send photographs to:

Ellie Dorsey
Conservation Law Foundation
3 Joy Street
Boston, MA 02108 USA

Catalogue:
Osborne, R., J. Calambokidis and E. Dorsey. 1988. A guide to marine mammals of Greater Puget Sound. Island Publishers, Anacortes, Washington.

SEI WHALE
Send photographs to:

Cetacean Research Unit
Box 159
Gloucester, MA 01930 USA

Catalogue:
No published catalogue.

RIGHT WHALE
Send photographs to:

North Atlantic Region:
  Scott Kraus
  c/o Right Whale Research Program
  New England Aquarium
  Central Wharf
  Boston, MA 02110 USA

South America:
  Long Term Research Institute
  191 Weston Road
  Lincoln, MA 01773 USA

South Africa:
  Peter Best
  Mammal Research Institute
  (Whale Unit)
  University of Pretoria
  c/o South African Museum
  P.O. Box 61
  Cape Town 8000
  South Africa

Australia:
  John Bannister
  Director
  Western Australia Museum
  Francis Street
  Perth 6000 Western Australia
  Australia

Catalogue:

Comprehensive research collections exist for eastern South America and South Africa. No published catalogue.

GRAY WHALE
Send photographs to:

  American Cetacean Society
  P.O. Box 2639
  San Pedro, CA 90731 USA

Catalogue:
No published catalogue.

KILLER WHALE
Send photographs to:

Pacific Ocean:
Marine Mammal Research Group
Pacific Biological Station
Fisheries and Oceans Canada
Nanaimo, British Columbia
Canada
V9R 5K6

Craig Matkin
North Gulf Oceanic Society
P.O. Box 15244
Homer, AK 99603 USA

Atlantic Ocean:
Whale Research Group
Memorial University of
Newfoundland
St. John's, Newfoundland
Canada
A1C 5S7

Allied Whale
College of the Atlantic
Bar Harbor, ME 04609 USA

Thomas Lyrholm
Department of Zoology
University of Stockholm
S106 91 Stockholm, Sweden

Johann Sigurjonsson
Marine Research Institute
Skulagata 4
Reykjavik, Iceland

Sea of Cortez:
Alejandro Acevedo
Marine Mammal Research
Program
Texas A & M University
P.O. Box 1675
Galveston, TX 77553 USA

Catalogues:
Bigg, M.A., G.M. Ellis, J.K.B. Ford,
and K.C. Balcomb. 1987. Killer
whales: a study of their identification, genealogy and natural history
in British Columbia and Washington
State. Phantom Press and Publishers,
Nanaimo, B.C. 79 pp.

Ellis, G. 1987. Killer whales of Prince
William Sound and Southeast Alaska:
a catalog of individuals photo-identified, 1976-1986. Technical Report No.
87-200, Sea World Research Institute,
Hubbs Marine Research Center, San
Diego, California, 76 pp.

SPERM WHALE
Send photographs and negatives to:

North Atlantic Ocean:
Tom Arnbom
Stockholms Universitet
Zoologiska Institutionen
5106 91
Stockholm, Sweden

Atlantic Ocean (Eastern North
America and Caribbean):
William A. Watkins
Woods Hole Oceanographic
Institution
Woods Hole, MA 02543 USA

Pacific Ocean:
Hal Whitehead
Department of Biology
Dalhousie University
Halifax, Nova Scotia
Canada
B3H 4J1

Catalogue:
No published catalogue.

BOTTLENOSE DOLPHIN
Send photographs to:

East Coast Populations:
Keith Rittmaster and
Victoria Thayer
North Carolina Maritime Museum
315 Front Street
Beaufort, NC 28516 USA

Florida:

Randall Wells
Conservation Biology
Brookfield Zoo
Chicago Zoological Society
Brookfield, IL 60513 USA

California:

R. H. Defran
Psychology Department
San Diego State University
San Diego, CA 92182 USA

Texas:

Bernd Würsig
Marine Mammal Research
Program
Texas A & M University
P.O. Box 1675
Galveston, TX 77553 USA

Catalogue:
No published catalogue.

WHITE-SIDED DOLPHIN
Send photographs to:

Cetacean Research Unit
Box 159
Gloucester, MA 01930 USA

BOWHEAD WHALE
Send photographs to:

David Rugh
National Marine Mammal
Laboratory/NOAA
Building 4
7600 Sand Point Way NE
Seattle, WA 98115 USA

Rolf Davis
LGL Ltd. Environmental
Research Assoc.
22 Fisher Street
P.O. Box 280
King City, Ontario
Canada
L0G 1K0

BRYDE'S WHALE
Send photographs to:

Pacific Ocean:

Bernie Tershy and Dawn Breese
Section of Neurobiology and
Behavior
Mudd Hall
Cornell University
Ithaca, NY 14853 USA

Atlantic Ocean:

William A. Watkins
Woods Hole Oceanographic
Institution
Woods Hole, MA 02543 USA

BELUGA
Send photographs to:

T.G. Smith
College of Renewable Resources
MacDonald College of McGill
University
21, 111 Bord de Lac
Ste. Anne de Bellevue, Quebec
Canada
H9X 1C0

RISSO'S DOLPHIN
Send photographs to:

Susan Kruse
Institute of Marine Sciences
University of California
Santa Cruz, CA 95064 USA

SPINNER DOLPHIN
Send photographs to:

Bernd Würsig
Marine Mammal Research
Program
Texas A & M University
P.O. Box 1675
Galveston, TX 77553 USA

APPENDIX II
Information Sources

WHERE TO OBTAIN MORE INFORMATION

(1) You can correspond directly with the researchers who maintain photographic identification catalogue/collections. If you have questions about specifics of photo-identifying a particular species, many researchers have indicated their willingness to supply advice. Most will acknowledge any materials you send them by letter or postcard.

(2) If you have questions about species not mentioned in this book or wish to determine if there is scientific interest in the photo-identification of other whales contact:

The American Cetacean Society
P.O. Box 2639
San Pedro, CA 90731 USA

Allied Whale
College of the Atlantic
Bar Harbor, ME 04609 USA

Whale Research Group
Memorial University of
Newfoundland
St. John's, Newfoundland
Canada
A1C 5S7

(3) The best single source for new information about whales for the general public is the *Whalewatcher*, published by:

The American Cetacean Society
P.O. Box 2639
San Pedro, California 90731 USA

Back issues of the *Whalewatcher* are available.

UPDATES

During the writing of this book we have been keenly aware of how rapidly the study of photographically-identified individual whales is growing. Research is being initiated on new species each year and some current projects or personnel may change. Thus we know that some of the information in this book will be out-of-date before long and there will be new information to add.

We would like to keep you current. Beginning in 1991, updated information can be obtained by sending $2.00 (Canadian or USA) to:

Photo-ID Guide Update
c/o Whale Research Group
Memorial University of
Newfoundland
St. John's, Newfoundland
Canada
A1C 5S7

Bibliography

POPULAR GENERAL BOOKS AND FIELD GUIDES ON WHALES

Baker, A. 1983. Whales and dolphins from New Zealand and Australia. Victoria University Press, Wellington, Australia. 133 pp.

Balcomb, K.C. and L. Foster. 1987. The whales of Hawaii. Marine Mammal Fund, San Francisco. 99 pp.

Bennett, B. 1983. The Oceanic Society field guide to the gray whale. Legacy Pub. Co., San Francisco. 50 pp.

Breton, M. 1986. Guide to watching whales in Canada. Department of Fisheries and Oceans, Ottawa. 54 pp.

Cousteau, J.Y. and Y. Paccalet. 1988. Whales. Harry N. Abrams, Inc., N.Y. 240 pp.

Darling, J. 1987. Wild whales: humpback, gray and killer whales. Publishers Group West, Emeryville, California. 96 pp.

Ellis, R. 1980. The book of whales. Alfred A. Knopf, New York. 202 pp.

Ellis, R. 1982. Dolphins and porpoises. Alfred A. Knopf, New York. 270 pp.

Ellis, R. 1982. A sea guide to marine mammals. American Cetacean Society, San Pedro, California. 26 pp.

Evans, P.G.H. 1987. Natural history of whales and dolphins. Facts on File Publications, New York. 343 pp.

Fontaine, P.H. 1988. Biologie and écologie des baleines de l'Atlantique Nord. S. Thibeault, 25 Place Marché Champlain, bureau 101, Quebec G1K 4H2. 185 pp.

Garrett, H. and C.K. Garrett. 1985. New England whales. Cape Ann Publishing Co., Gloucester, Massachusetts. 36 pp.

Gaskin, D.E. 1982. The ecology of whales and dolphins. Heinemann, London and Exeter, New Hampshire. 459 pp.

Golden, F. (ed.). 1989. Whither the whales? Oceanus 32(1):1-144. This special issue, containing 18 articles on whales, can be ordered from Oceanus, 93 Water St., Woods Hole, Massachusetts 02543. Price is $5.50.

Haley, D. (ed.). 1986. Marine mammals. Revised edition. Pacific Search Press, Seattle. 295 pp.

Harrison, R. and M.M. Bryden. 1988. Whales, dolphins and porpoises. Facts on File Publications, New York. 240 pp.

Hoyt, E. 1984. The whale watcher's handbook. Penguin Books Canada, Ltd., Markham, Ontario. 245 pp.

Hoyt, E. 1984. The whales of Canada. Camden House Publishing, Ltd., Camden East, Ontario. 128 pp.

Katona, S., V. Rough and D.T. Richardson. 1983. A field guide to the whales, porpoises and seals of the Gulf of Maine and Eastern Canada, Cape Cod to Newfoundland. Charles Scribner's Sons, New York. 256 pp.

Leatherwood, S., D.K. Caldwell and H.E. Winn. 1976. Whales, dolphins and porpoises of the Western North Atlantic: A guide to their identification. NOAA Technical Report, NMFS Circular 396, U.S. Department of Commerce, Washington, D.C. 176 pp.

Leatherwood, S., R.R. Reeves, W.R. Perrin and W.E. Evans. 1988. Whales, dolphins and porpoises of the Eastern North Pacific and adjacent arctic waters: A guide to their identification. Dover Pub., New York. 245 pp. (Reprint of NOAA Technical Report, NMFS Circular 444, U.S. Department of Commerce, Washington, D.C.).

Leatherwood, S., R. Reeves and L. Foster. 1983. The Sierra Club handbook of whales and dolphins. Sierra Club Books, San Francisco. 302 pp.

Lien, J., L. Fawcett and S. Staniforth. 1985. Wet and fat: Whales and seals of Newfoundland and Labrador. Breakwater Books, St.John's, Newfoundland. 136 pp.

MacDonald, D. 1984. The encyclopedia of mammals. Facts on File Publications, New York. See pp. 162-230 on cetaceans.

Mallory, K. and A. Conley. 1989. Rescue of the stranded whales. Simon and Schuster books for Young Readers, New York. 63 pp.

Minasian, S., K. Balcomb and L. Foster. 1984. The world's whales: the complete illustrated guide. W.W. Norton and Co., New York; London. 224 pp.

Orr, R.T. and R.C. Helm. 1989. Marine mammals of California. Revised edition. University of California Press, Berkeley. 93 pp.

Osborne, R., J. Calambokidis and E. Dorsey. 1988. A guide to marine mammals of Greater Puget Sound. Island Publishers, Anacortes, Washington. 191 pp.

Reeves, R.R. and E. Mitchell. 1987. Cetaceans of Canada. Underwater World Factsheet 59. Minister of Supply and Services, Canada, Fs 41-33/59-1987E. 27 pp. This publication is also available in French.

Ridgway, S.H. and R. Harrison (eds.). 1981-89. Handbook of marine mammals. Vol. 1-4. Academic Press, New York. 442 pp.

Taylor, S. (ed.). 1989. The world's whales-A closer look. Selected Papers from the Third Biennial Conference and Symposium. The American Cetacean Society, San Pedro, California. 197 pp.

ARTICLES ON PHOTO-IDENTIFICATION

These articles provide examples of how photo-identification is providing important information on the biology of selected marine mammals. We hope you will consult some of them in order to learn more about particular topics or species. You may need to ask your librarian for help in finding some of these references.

References marked by (P) are popular, easily readable articles; those marked by (T) are technical or scientific in nature; and those marked by (A) are abstracts, brief summaries of research results prepared for professional meetings. Note that abstracts usually do not contain the data on which their conclusions are based; consequently, such contributions should not be relied upon with the same confidence as papers or books that have been reviewed by scientists during the publication process. Photo-copies of individual abstracts mentioned below may be obtained from Allied Whale, College of the Atlantic, Bar Harbor, Maine, USA 04609, for $2.00 each, postpaid.

GENERAL

Bigg, M.A., G.M. Ellis and K.C. Balcomb. 1986. The photographic identification of individual cetaceans. Whalewatcher 20(2):10-12. (P)

Hammond, P.S., S.A. Mizroch and G.P. Donovan (eds.). 1990. Individual recognition and the estimation of cetacean population parameters. Rep. int. Whal. Commn. (special issue 12). Readers should note that this important volume contains approximately 50 scientific papers on different aspects of photo-ID studies. (T)

Hammond, P.S. 1986. Estimating the size of naturally marked whale populations using capture-recapture techniques. Rep. int. Whal. Commn. (special issue 8), pp. 253-282. (T)

Gordon, J.C.D., V. Papastavrou and A. Alling. 1985. Measuring blue whales: a photogrammetric method. Cetus 6(2):5-8. (P)

Katona, S.K. 1989. Getting to know you. Oceanus 39(1):37-44. Readers should note that this Spring, 1989, issue of Oceanus, contains nearly 20 articles on whales, dolphins and porpoises. (P)

Pennycuick, C.J. 1978. Identification using natural markings. pp. 147-159. In: B. Stonehouse (ed.), Animal marking: Recognizing marking in animals in research, MacMillan Press, London. (T)

HUMPBACK WHALE

Baker, C.S., L.M. Herman, A.A. Wolman, H.E. Winn, J. Hall, G. Kaufman, J. Reinke and J. Ostman. 1986. The migratory movement and population structure of humpback whales (*Megaptera novaeangliae*) in the central and eastern North Pacific. Marine Ecology-Progress Series 31:105-119. (T)

Clapham, P.J. and D.K. Mattila. 1988. Observations of migratory transits of two humpback whales. Marine Mammal Science 4(1):59-61. (P,T)

Clapham, P.J. and C.A. Mayo. 1987. Reproduction and recruitment of individually identified humpback whales, *Megaptera novaeangliae*, observed in Massachusetts Bay, 1979-1985. Can. J. Zoology 65:2853-2863. (T)

Chu, K.C. and S.L. Nieukirk. 1985. Dorsal fin shapes and scars as indicators of sex, age and social status in humpback whales (*Megaptera novaeangliae*). Abstracts: Sixth Biennial Conference on the Biology of Marine Mammals, Vancouver, November 1985. p. 22. (A)

Glockner, D.A. 1983. Determining the sex of humpback whales (*Megaptera novaeangliae*) in their natural environment. pp. 447-464. In: R. Payne (ed.), Communication and behavior of whales. Westview Press, Boulder, Colorado. (T)

Glockner, D.A. and S.C. Venus. 1983. Identification, growth rate, and behavior of humpback whale (*Megaptera novaeangliae*) cows and calves in the waters of Maui, Hawaii, 1977-1979. pp. 223-258. In: R. Payne (ed.), Communication and behavior of whales. Westview Press, Boulder, Colorado. (T)

Katona, S., B. Baxter, O. Brazier, S. Kraus, J. Perkins and H. Whitehead. 1979. Identification of humpback whales by fluke photographs. pp. 33-44. In: H.E. Winn and B.L. Olla (eds.), Behavior of marine animals, Vol.3: Cetaceans, Plenum Press, New York. (T)

Katona, S.K. and H.P. Whitehead. 1981. Identifying humpback whales using their natural markings. Polar Record 20:439-444. (T)

Kaufman, G.D. and P.H. Forestell. 1986. Hawaii's humpback whales. Pacific Whale Foundation Press, Maui, Hawaii. 176 pp. (P)

Stone, G.S., S.K. Katona and E. Tucker. 1986. Humpback whales half-way at Bermuda. Whalewatcher 20(2):3-7. (P)

Weinrich, M.T. 1989. Social development of humpback whales in the southern Gulf of Maine. Abstracts: Eighth Biennial Conference on the Biology of Marine Mammals, Monterey, California, December 1989. p. 71. (A)

Williamson, J.M. 1985. Humpback whale research in the Gulf of St. Lawrence. Whalewatcher 19(3):9-11. (P)

Winn, L.K. and H.E. Winn. 1985. Wings in the sea: The humpback whale. University Press of New England, Hanover, New Hampshire. (P)

BLUE WHALE

Calambokidis, J., S. Kruse, J.C. Cubbage, R. Wells, K.C. Balcomb, D. Ewald and G. Steiger. 1987. Blue whale occurrence and photo-identification along the central California coast. Abstracts: Seventh Biennial Conference on the Biology of Marine Mammals, Miami, December 1987. p. 8. (A)

Calambokidis, J., G.H. Stieger, J.C. Cubbage, K.C. Balcomb, P. Bloedel and D.W. Bockus. 1989. Abundance and distribution of blue and humpback whales in the Gulf of the Farallones, California. Abstracts: Eighth Biennial Conference on the Biology of Marine Mammals, Monterey, California, December 1989. p. 10. (A)

Sears, R. 1987. Photographic identification of individual blue whales (Balaenoptera musculus) in the Sea of Cortez. Cetus 7(1):14-17. (P)

Sears, R., F.W. Wenzel and J.M. Willamson. 1987. The blue whale: a catalogue of individuals from the western North Atlantic (Gulf of St. Lawrence). Mingan Islands Cetacean Study, St. Lambert, Quebec, Canada. (T)

Small, G.L. 1971. The blue whale. Columbia University Press, New York. (P)

Wenzel, F., D.K. Mattila and P.J. Clapham. 1988. Balaenoptera musculus in the Gulf of Maine. Marine Mammal Science 4(2):172-175. (T)

FINBACK WHALE

Agler, B.A. and S.K. Katona. 1987. Photo-identification of individual finback whales. Whalewatcher 21(3):3-6. (P)

Agler, B.A., J.A. Beard, R.S. Bowman, S.E. Frohock, S.K. Katona, K.A. Robertson and I. Seipt. 1989. Fin whale, Balaenoptera physalus, photographic identification: preliminary results from the Gulf of Maine. Abstracts: Eighth Biennial Conference on the Biology of Marine Mammals, Monterey, California, December 1989. p.1. (A)

Mattila, D.K., C. Carlson, P.J. Clapham and C.A. Mayo. 1983. Resightings of individually identifiable fin whales in the waters of Stellwagen Bank and Cape Cod Bay, Massachusetts. Abstracts: Fifth Biennial Conference on the Biology of Marine Mammals, Boston, November 1983. p. 100. (T)

Mayo, C.A., M.P. Hawvermale and C.A. Carlson. 1985. Identification of individual fin whales: the technique and its use. Abstracts: Sixth Biennial Conference on the Biology of Marine Mammals, Vancouver, November 1985. p. 36. (T)

MINKE WHALE

Dorsey, E.M. 1983. Exclusive adjoining ranges in individually identified minke whales (*Balaenoptera acutorostrata*) in Washington State. Canadian Journal of Zoology 61(1):174-181. (T)

Hoelzel, A.R., E.M. Dorsey and S.J. Stern. 1985. Specialist foraging in the minke whale (*Balaenoptera acutorostrata*). Abstracts: Sixth Biennial Conference on the Biology of Marine Mammals, Vancouver, November 1985. p. 38. (T)

RIGHT WHALE

Dorf, B.A., H.E. Winn, R.D. Kenney and G.O. Klein. 1989. Distributional ecology of the North Atlantic right whale (*Eubalaena glacialis*) based on photographic identification of individuals. Abstracts: Eighth Biennial Conference on the Biology of Marine Mammals, Monterey, California, December 1989. p. 16. (A)

Gilmore, M. and C. Danton 1985. Identification of North Atlantic right whales. pp. 56-57. In: C. Mayo, C. Carlson, P. Clapham and D. Mattila (eds.), Humpback whales of the

Southern Gulf of Maine. Center for Coastal Studies, Provincetown, Massachusetts. (P)

Knowlton, A.R. and S.D. Kraus. 1989. Calving intervals, rates and success in North Atlantic right whales. Abstracts: Eighth Biennial Conference on the Biology of Marine Mammals, Monterey, California, December 1989. p. 35. (A)

Kraus, S.D. 1987. A move to the right: A collaborative effort for the rarest whale. Whalewatcher 21(3):14-15. (P)

Kraus, S.D., K.E. Moore, C.A. Price, M.J. Crone, W.A. Watkins, H.E. Winn and J.H. Prescott. 1987. The use of photographs to identify individual North Atlantic right whales (*Eubalaena glacialis*). Rep. int. Whal. Commn. (special issue 10):145-152. (T)

Kraus, S.D., J.H. Prescott and G. Stone. 1983. Right whales in the northern Gulf of Maine. Whalewatcher 17(4):18-21. (P)

Payne, R. 1986. Long term behavioral studies of the southern right whale (*Eubalaena australis*). Rep. int. Whal. Commn. (special issue 10):161-167. (T)

Payne, R.S. 1972. Swimming with Patagonia's right whales. National Geographic Magazine 142: 576-587. (P)

Payne, R., O. Brazier, E.M. Dorsey, J.S. Perkins, V.J. Rowntree and A. Titus. 1983. External features in southern right whales (*Eubalaena australis*) and their use in identifying individuals. pp. 371-445. In: R. Payne (ed.), Communication and behavior of whales, Westview Press, Boulder, Colorado.(T)

Payne, R.S., J. Seger, V.J. Rowntree and J.S. Perkins. 1989. Persistent association of mothers and female offspring in the southern right whale (*Eubalaena australis*). Abstracts: Eighth Biennial Conference on the Biology of Marine Mammals, Monterey, California, December 1989. p. 49. (A)

GRAY WHALE

Bryant, P.J. and S.K. Lafferty. 1983. Photo-identification of gray whales. Whalewatcher 17(1): 6-9. (P)

Darling, J.D. 1984. Gray whales off Vancouver Island, British Columbia. pp. 267-287. In: M.L. Jones, S.L. Swartz and S. Leatherwood, (eds.), The Gray Whale, *Eschrichtius robustus*. Academic Press, N.Y. (T)

Hatler, D.F. and J.D. Darling. 1974. Recent observations of the gray whale in British Columbia. Canadian Field Naturalist 88:449-459. (P,T)

Swartz, S. 1986. Gray whale migratory, social and breeding behavior. Rep. int. Whal. Commn. (special issue 8):207-230. (T)

BOWHEAD WHALE

Nerini, M.D., H.W. Braham, W.M. Marquette and D.J. Rugh. 1984. Life history of the bowhead whale, *Balaena mysticetus*. (Mammalia: cetacea) Journal of Zoology, London 204:443-468. (T)

Rugh, D.J. 1985. Bowhead whale individual identification through aerial photography. Abstracts: Sixth Biennial Conference on the Biology of Marine Mammals, Vancouver, November 1985. p. 67. (A)

Rugh, D.J. 1987. Bowhead whales re-identified through aerial photography. Abstracts: Seventh Biennial Conference on the Biology of Marine Mammals, Miami, December 1987, p. 59. (A).

KILLER WHALE

Bigg, M., I. MacAskie and G. Ellis. 1983. Photo-identification of individual killer whales. Whalewatcher 17(1):3-5 (P).

Bigg, M.A., G.M. Ellis, J.K.B. Ford and K.C. Balcomb. 1987. Killer whales. A study of their identification, geneology and natural history in British Columbia and Washington State. Phantom Press and Publishers, Inc., Nanaimo, British Columbia. 79 pp. (P,T)

Chandler, R., C. Goebel and K. Balcomb. 1977. Who is that killer whale? A new key to whale watching. Whalewatcher 11(3):10-12 (P).

Ellis, G. (ed.). 1984. Killer whales of southern Alaska. A catalogue of individuals photo-identified in 1984. Hubbs Sea World Research Institute Tech. Rep. 84-176. 73 pp. (P)

Hoyt, E. 1981. Orca, the whale called "killer." E.P. Dutton, New York. (P)

Hoyt, E. 1984. The whales called "killer." National Geographic Magazine 166: 220-237. (P)

Lichter, A.A., I. Bessinga and A.R. Hoelzel. 1989. Home range of individually identified killer whales in Argentina. Abstracts: Eighth Biennial Conference on the Biology of Marine Mammals, Monterey, California, December 1989. p. 38. (A)

Sigurjonnson, J. and S. Leatherwood, (eds.). 1988. North Atlantic killer whales. Rit. Fiskideildar (Journal of the Marine Research Institute, Reykjavik) Vol. 11. 316 pp. Readers should note that this volume contains over 20 articles on killer whales, including several studies based on photo-identification. (T)

SPERM WHALE

Arnbom, T. 1987. Individual identification of sperm whales. Rep. int. Whal. Commn. 37:201-204. (T)

Arnbom, T. 1987. Sperm whales off the Galapagos Islands. Whalewatcher 21(2):9-12. (P)

Gordon, J.C.D. 1987. Sperm whale groups and social behavior observed off Sri Lanka. Rep. int. Whal. Commn. 37:205-217. (T)

Whitehead, H. and T. Arnbom. 1987. Social organization of sperm whales off the Galapagos Islands, February-April, 1985. Canadian Journal of Zoology 65:913-919. (T)

Whitehead, H. and S. Waters. 1989. Social organization and population structure of sperm whales off the Galapagos Islands, Ecuador. Abstracts: Eighth Biennial Conference on the Biology of Marine Mammals, Monterey, California, December 1989. p. 72. (A)

BOTTLENOSE DOLPHIN

Defran, R.H. and D.W. Weller. 1989. Pacific coast bottlenose dolphins: dramatic shifts in abundance, school size and resight patterns. Abstracts: Eighth Biennial Conference on the Biology of Marine Mammals, Monterey, California, December 1989. p. 15. (A)

Schultz, G.M., R.H. Defran and M.A. Espinoza Ley. 1985. A method for analyzing dorsal fin photographs in *Tursiops truncatus*. Abstracts: Sixth Biennial Conference on the Biology of Marine Mammals, Vancouver, November 1985. p. 70 (A).

Shane, S. 1988. The bottlenose dolphin in the wild. Hatcher Trade Press, San Carlos, California. (P)

Weigle, B.L. 1985. Movements of naturally marked bottlenosed dolphins in Southern Tampa Bay, Florida. Abstracts: Sixth Biennial Conference on the Biology of Marine Mammals, Vancouver, November 1985. p. 79. (A)

Wells, R. 1985. Bottlenose dolphin social behavior: longterm research in a natural laboratory. Whalewatcher 19(4):3-6. (P)

Wells, R.S. 1989. Secrets of high society. National Wildlife, Aug.-Sept. 1989, pp. 38-44. (P)

OTHER SPECIES

Black, N. 1989. The behavior of Pacific white-sided dolphins (*Lagenorhynchus obliquidens*) in Monterey Bay, California. Abstracts: Eighth Biennial Conference on the Biology of Marine Mammals, Monterey, California, December 1989. p. 7. (A)

Breese, D. and B. Tershy. 1988. Bryde's whales and El Niño in the Gulf of California. Whalewatcher 22(3):6-9. (P)

Byrnes, P.E., N.A. Black and S. Leatherwood. Photo-identification, behavior and distribution of spotted dolphins (*Stenella frontalis*) in the Bahama Banks. Abstracts: Eighth Biennial Conference on the Biology of Marine Mammals, Monterey, California, December 1989. p. 10. (A)

Caron, L. and T.G. Smith. 1985. Preliminary results on the status and behaviour of a hunted herd of belugas (*Delphinapterus leucas*) in Eastern Hudson Bay. Abstracts: Sixth Biennial Conference on the Biology of Marine Mammals, Vancouver, November 1985. p. 20. (A)

Jenner, C., M. N. Jenner and P.H. Forestell. 1989. Repeated behavioral observation of six photo-identified adult pygmy killer whales during one month prior to stranding by three members of the pod. Abstracts: Eighth Biennial Conference on the Biology of Marine Mammals, Monterey, California, December 1989. p. 31. (A)

Kruse, S. 1987. Behavior of Risso's dolphins in Monterey Bay, California. Abstracts: Seventh Biennial Conference on the Biology of Marine Mammals, Miami, December 1987. p. 39. (A)

Kruse, S. 1989. Behavior of Risso's dolphins in Monterey Bay, California. Abstracts: Eighth Biennial Conference on the Biology of Marine Mammals, Monterey, California, December 1989. p. 36. (A)

Weinrich, M.T., C.R. Belt, M.R. Schilling and M. Marcy. 1987. Behavior of sei whales in the southern Gulf of Maine, Summer 1986. Whalewatcher 20(4):4-7. (P)

Würsig, B., R.S. Wells and M. Würsig. 1983. Association and movement patterns of recognizable Hawaiian spinner dolphins. Abstracts: Fifth Biennial Conference on the Biology of Marine Mammals, Boston, November 1983. p. 109. (A)

Glossary of Whale Words

Baleen: Fibrous plates constructed of keratin, material much like human fingernails, grows from the roof of the mouth of some species of whales; used to filter small food organisms from the water.

Barnacle: A marine crustacean that attaches itself to rocks, ship bottoms, certain whales, etc.

Beak: The snout, or forward projecting jaws of a cetacean; term used primarily with dolphins and porpoises.

Benthic: Pertaining to the sea bottom or to organisms that live in or on the sea bottom.

Blow: The visible breath of a whale, consisting of water vapour and droplets.

Blowhole: The nostrils of a cetacean, usually located on the top of the head; two blowholes in Mysticeti, one blowhole in Odontoceti.

Bowriding: The behaviour in dolphins and porpoises involving swimming in the bowwave created by moving boats or large whales.

Breaching: The behaviour in cetaceans that involves thrusting most or all of the body out of the water and landing with a large splash.

Bull: An adult male whale.

Calf: A baby whale.

Callosity: Rough, lumpy protrusions on the top and front of the head of right whales; made of keratin.

Caudal: Of, pertaining to, or near the tail or posterior part of the body.

Cetacean: A marine mammal of the order of Cetacea, which includes whales, dolphins, and porpoises.

Chevron: A pigmentation pattern shaped like the letter V on the back of a finback whale.

Cow: An adult female whale.

Crustacean: Of the class Crustacea, breathes through gills and has a body commonly covered by a hard shell; includes barnacles, crab, shrimp, lobster, amphipods, and copepods, among others.

Dolphin: Sometimes used interchangeably with "porpoise," but generally defined as having a beak, conical-shaped teeth, and a falcate dorsal fin.

Dorsal: Of, toward, on, in or near the top.

Dorsal fin: The top fin in marine vertebrates.

Echolocation: To orient, navigate, or find food by making sounds and listening for echoes reflecting from objects.

Falcate: Curved and tapering; sickle shaped.

Flippers: The limbs of marine mammals, including cetaceans pinnipeds, manatees, and dugongs.

Flipper slapping: The behaviour in cetaceans that involves raising the pectoral fin out of the water and slapping it on the surface.

Flukes: The horizontally oriented tail fin of cetaceans; flukes are strong, fibrous but contain no bones.

Krill: Term in general use to describe small, shrimplike crustaceans eaten by many baleen whales.

Lob-tailing: The behaviour in cetaceans that involves raising the flukes out of the water and slapping them on the surface.

Mammal: A vertebrate animal characterized by warmbloodedness, hair, lungs, nursing young, and giving live birth.

Melon: The bulbous forehead of Odontocete cetaceans, which contains oil and is thought to be involved in sound projection.

Mysticeti: The order of baleen whales, from the Greek *mystax* (moustache) and *cetus* (whale).

Odontoceti: The order of toothed whales, from the Greek *odous* (tooth) and *cetus* (whale).

Pectoral fin: The flippers or forelimbs of cetaceans.

Peduncle: A stalk; in cetaceans, the tail stock between the anus and the fluke.

Pelagic: Of, pertaining to, or living in the open ocean far from land.

Pinniped: An order of aquatic, carnivorous mammals that includes sea lions, true seals, and walruses; from the Latin *pinna* (feather) and *pes* (foot), or "featherfoot."

Plankton: The marine animal and plant organisms that drift or float with wind and currents, waves, etc. in the upper layers of the sea.

Pod: A group of two or more whales.

Porpoise: Sometimes used interchangeably with "dolphin," but generally defined as having a short beak or no beak at all, spade-shaped teeth, and a triangular dorsal fin.

Rorqual: Any of several baleen whales of the genus *Balaenoptera* having numerous longitudinal grooves on the lower surface of the body, and a dorsal fin.

Rostrum: The jaws of a baleen whale elongated ("telescoped") forward to enlarge the mouth cavity.

Spout: A column of spray thrown into the air by a whale when breathing.

Spyhopping: The behaviour in cetaceans that involves raising the head vertically out of the water, then sinking back into the water without causing much splash.

Terminal dive: Deep dive at the end of a series of shallow dives, when flukes are most likely to be seen.

Ventral: Of, pertaining to, or situated on or near the belly or abdomen; on the lower surface of the body.

Ventral pleats: The longitudinal grooves on the undersurface of certain species of baleen whales.

Whale lice: Crustaceans in the family Cyamidae, generally yellowish-white or yellowish-orange, that live on certain species of cetaceans.

Whale Anatomy

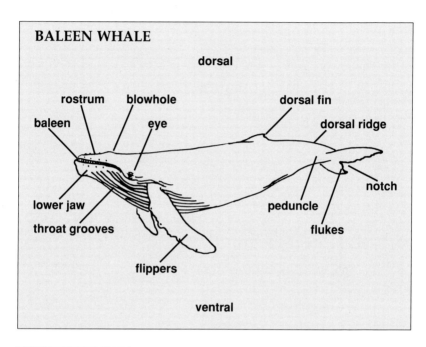

BALEEN WHALE

dorsal

rostrum blowhole   dorsal fin

baleen   eye   dorsal ridge

lower jaw   notch

throat grooves   peduncle

flukes

flippers

ventral

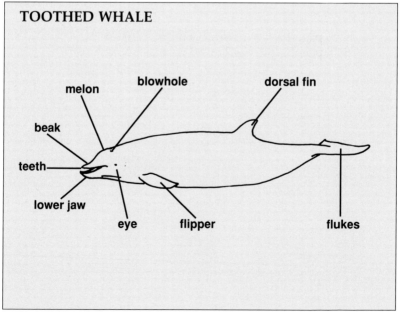

TOOTHED WHALE

melon blowhole   dorsal fin

beak

teeth

lower jaw

eye   flipper   flukes

Drawings by Robin Makowski

PHOTO CREDITS

Humpback whales: Allied Whale; Whale Research Group,
   Memorial University of Newfoundland
Blue whales: Mingan Island Cetacean Study
Finback whales: Allied Whale
Minke whales: Eleanor Dorsey
Sei whales: Cetacean Research Unit
Right whales: New England Aquarium, Long Term Research
   Institute
Gray whales: Susan Lafferty
Killer whales: Graeme Ellis
Sperm whales: Hal Whitehead
Bottlenose dolphins: Randall S. Wells
Bowhead whales: David Rugh
Bryde's whales: Bernie Tershy, Dawn Breese
Risso's dolphins: Susan Kruse
Spinner dolphins: Bernd Würsig
Back cover photos: Lura Cenzano

ANSWERS

Answer from page 15: Photos 6 and 9 match.
Answer from page 17: Photos 2 and 5 match.